The Best Book of
Sharks

Claire Llewellyn

KINGFISHER
NEW YORK

Contents

Author: Claire Llewellyn
Consultant: Brian Harris,
London Zoo Aquarium
Illustrators: Ray Grinaway,
Roger Stewart

KINGFISHER
LONDON & NEW YORK

Text copyright © Kingfisher 1999
Published in the United States by Kingfisher,
175 Fifth Ave., New York, NY 10010
Kingfisher is an imprint of
Macmillan Children's Books, London.
All rights reserved.

Distributed in the U.S. and Canada by Macmillan,
175 Fifth Ave., New York, NY 10010

LIBRARY OF CONGRESS CATALOGING-IN-PUBLICATION DATA
Llewellyn, Claire.
The best book of sharks / by Claire Llewellyn.—1st ed.
p.   cm.
Published simultaneously under the title: My best book
of sharks.
Includes index.
Summary: Introduces the world of sharks, examining
their characteristics, breeding, life cycle, and behavior
and describing various species.
   1. Sharks Juvenile literature.   [1. Sharks.]   I. Title.
QL638.9.L57   1999
597.3—dc21   99-12760   CIP

ISBN 978-0-7534-5875-4

Kingfisher books are available for special promotions
and premiums. For details contact: Special Markets
Department, Macmillan, 175 Fifth Ave., New York,
NY 10010.

For more information, please visit
www.kingfisherbooks.com

Printed in China
15
15TR/0215/WKT/MAR/128MA

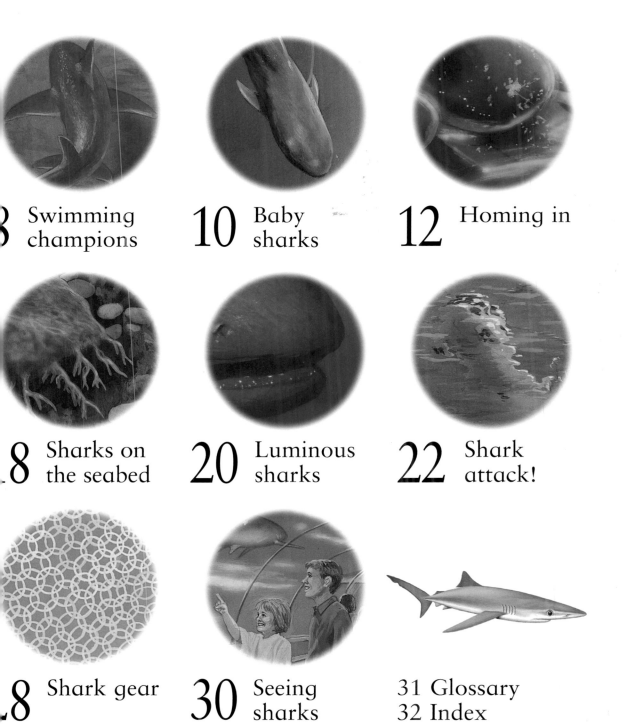

Meet the shark

The shark is one of the fastest fish in the sea. Every part of its body is perfect for the water—its light, flexible skeleton, its smooth, sleek shape, and its powerful fins and tail. These features mean some sharks are deadly hunters. Not all sharks are fast and fierce, though. Some, such as the whale shark, are gentle giants that feed only on the tiniest creatures in the sea.

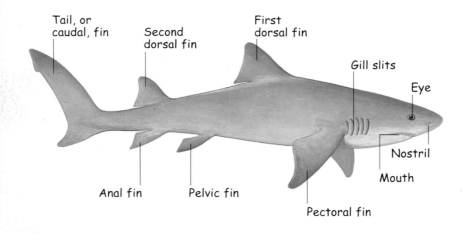

Tail, or caudal, fin

Second dorsal fin

First dorsal fin

Gill slits

Eye

Nostril

Mouth

Anal fin

Pelvic fin

Pectoral fin

A shark's body

Most fish have skeletons made of hard bone, but a shark's skeleton is made of light, flexible cartilage. This allows the shark to twist and turn very quickly. Like all fish, sharks use their gills to take in oxygen from the water.

Gray reef shark hunting for prey over a coral reef

A world of sharks

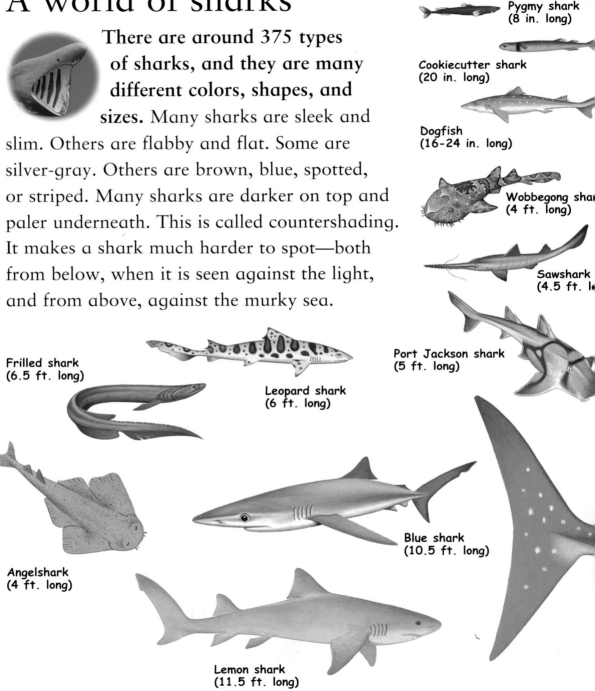

There are around 375 types of sharks, and they are many different colors, shapes, and sizes. Many sharks are sleek and slim. Others are flabby and flat. Some are silver-gray. Others are brown, blue, spotted, or striped. Many sharks are darker on top and paler underneath. This is called countershading. It makes a shark much harder to spot—both from below, when it is seen against the light, and from above, against the murky sea.

Pygmy shark
(8 in. long)

Cookiecutter shark
(20 in. long)

Dogfish
(16-24 in. long)

Wobbegong shark
(4 ft. long)

Sawshark
(4.5 ft. long)

Frilled shark
(6.5 ft. long)

Leopard shark
(6 ft. long)

Port Jackson shark
(5 ft. long)

Angelshark
(4 ft. long)

Blue shark
(10.5 ft. long)

Lemon shark
(11.5 ft. long)

Zebra shark
(11.5 ft. long

Mako shark
(12.5 ft. long)

Great hammerhead
shark (13 ft. long)

Thresher shark
(15 ft. long)

Tiger shark
(16.5 ft. long)

Great white shark
(20 ft. long)

ale shark
ft. long)

7

Swimming champions

A shark hardly seems to move as it swims along. It simply flicks its tail from side to side to push its body through the water. It uses its fins to turn, stop, rise, or dive. Most fish have soft, bendable fins that can be stretched out or tucked back. A shark's fins are stiff and stick out like paddles, and cannot be folded away.

Gray smooth hound sharks swimming along the seabed

Shark skin

Most sharks' skin is covered with tiny, thorny teeth called denticles. If you stroked the skin from back to front, it could cut your hand.

Shark tails

Shark tails have different shapes. Bull and thresher sharks have long, streamlined tails that slice through the water so that the sharks can twist and turn quickly. The swell shark's broader tail gently wafts the water so that the fish can cruise along the seabed. The balanced shape of the great white's tail allows it—and others like it—to swim the fastest of all.

Thresher shark

Great white shark

Bull shark

Swell shark

Baby sharks

Baby sharks are known as pups, and they grow in different ways. Most grow from eggs in their mother's body, and are born into the sea. Others grow from eggs that are laid in the water. Each egg sits in a case, which hardens t protect the growing pup. The shark hatches ou when it is almost fully grown, and swims off to hide somewhere safe. It must then take care of itself—the mother leaves it on its own.

Hammerhead shark pups

Born into the sea

Shark pups slip out through an opening in their mother's body. They are joined to their mother by tiny cords, which break as the pups swim away.

Lemon shark pups

Cat shark eggcase and pup

Horn shark eggcase and pup

Dogfish eggcases (also called mermaid's purses)

hark eggcases

gcases are tough and
lt to last. A cat shark's
gcase has tiny tendrils
t cling tightly to plants.

A horn shark's eggcase
survives in cracks in the
rocks. Other eggcases settle
on the seabed. Many are
eaten before the pups hatch.

Tendrils of
cat shark's
eggcase wraps
around plant

Dogfish pup
(4 in. long)

Yolk
sac

Dogfish ready
to hatch

Dogfish eggs

Dogfish lay around 20 eggs, often in a
clump of seaweed. Each egg contains a
yolk sac for the pup to feed on as it grows.
The eggs take nine months to hatch. The
pups look just like their parents, but smaller.

11

Homing in

Sharks are very good at finding their prey in the vast, dark world of the ocean. They can feel movement in the water from far away. They can smell the faintest whiff of blood. They can even pick up the electrical signals from an animal's beating heart. Most sharks prefer to hunt alone, but sometimes a group will attack the same prey. The sharks snap wildly and even bite one another in a savage feeding frenzy.

Eye

Nostril

Hammerhead hunter

A hammerhead shark has an eye and a nostril on each end of its hammer-shaped head. As it swims, it swings its head from side to side to pick up signals from the water.

Gray reef sharks attack a tuna in a feeding frenzy

The deadly jaws

Sharks feed on almost every creature in the sea. They catch penguins, seals, turtles, fish, and crabs. Because different types of sharks feed on different types of foods, they have different-shaped jaws and teeth. A few teeth drop out during every meal, but new ones move up to take their place. A shark goes through hundreds of teeth during its lifetime.

Shaken to pieces
Sharks cannot chew. If a meal is too large to swallow whole, they shake it from side to side to tear it into chunks.

Ragged teeth
The sandtiger shark (also known as the ragged tooth or gray nurse shark) has several rows of sharp, spiky teeth. Each tooth is around 1.5 inches long.

ypes of teeth

shark's teeth are a toolkit
r catching and cutting up
od. Long, spiky teeth can
ewer a slithery octopus or
uid. Serrated teeth can
w through bony fish.
ard, flat teeth can grind
shellfish, such as lobsters
d crabs, and even crunch
rough a tough turtle shell.

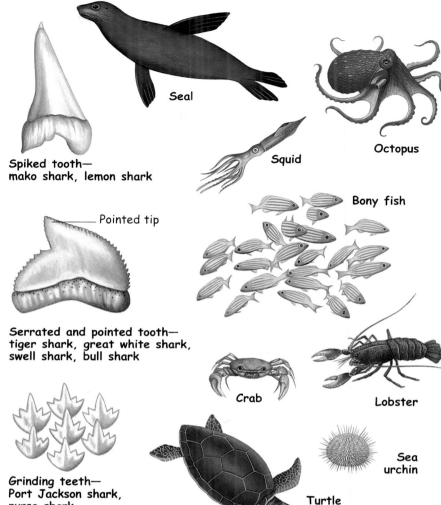

Seal

Octopus

Squid

**Spiked tooth—
mako shark, lemon shark**

— Pointed tip

Bony fish

**Serrated and pointed tooth—
tiger shark, great white shark,
swell shark, bull shark**

Crab

Lobster

**Grinding teeth—
Port Jackson shark,
nurse shark**

Sea
urchin

Turtle

**Sandtiger shark
(10 ft. long)**

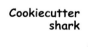

Cookiecutter
shark

Lips form a round
sucker that grabs
hold of prey

A cookiecutter bite

A cookiecutter shark's jaws
are perfectly round, like
a cookie cutter. When it
sinks its teeth into a seal
or whale, it tears out a
cookie-shaped mouthful.

15

Gentle giants

The whale shark is the world's biggest fish, yet it feeds on minuscule creatures. As the shark cruises along near the surface of the ocean, it sucks in great mouthfuls of water. This pours through curtains of long, fine bristles that hang inside the shark's mouth. The bristles work like a filter or sieve, trapping schools of plankton and tiny fish, which the shark then swallows.

Whale shark teeth

Tiny teeth

Whale and basking sharks have tiny teeth, around half the size of your little fingernail. They do not use them to bite or crush their food, but to help them spitit out from time to time.

Basking sharks
Basking sharks swim along with their mouths wide open, trapping tiny sea creatures such as shrimp and plankton.

Plankton
Plankton is the name given to the tiny creatures that drift in the sea. You can only see them under a microscope.

Sharks on the seabed

Some sharks hide at the bottom of the sea to rest or pounce on their prey. Their flat bodies, brown skin, and blotchy markings help them blend in with the stones and sand. One shark, the wobbegong, has frills of skin around its mouth. These look so much like pieces of seaweed that small fish swim up to nibble them and end up being eaten themselves.

Taking a break

Port Jackson sharks like to feed at night. They spend t day resting in sandy caves in gaps between the rocks.

The wobbegong shark waiting for its next meal

ngel in the sand

  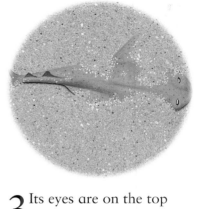

The angelshark spends
. much of its life resting
d feeding on the seabed.

2 It flaps its fins to cover
itself with sand. It is
now almost invisible.

3 Its eyes are on the top
of its head so that it can
stay on the lookout for food.

Luminous sharks

Some sharks that live in deep, dark water have special ways of using light. The massive mouth of a megamouth shark shines with a silvery glow. This may attract the tasty schools of plankton that megamouths like to eat. The cookiecutter shark also uses light. Its belly glows a luminous green. This may attract a nearby animal, such as a whale, that is large enough to bite.

Bright lanterns

Lantern sharks swim in large schools. Each fish is covered with a luminous slime that glows in the dark. Scientists believe that this glowing slime may help the fish keep their place in the school.

Megamouth sharks live in such deep water that only six or so have ever been found

Shark attack!

DO: Tuck legs up and keep as still and quiet as possible

Some sharks can be dangerous to humans. Around 30 types of sharks, including the bull shark, tiger shark, and great white shark, have attacked people in the water. Some have even overturned sailboats. Large, meat-eating sharks have powerful jaws, and when they attack they often kill. However, shark attacks are very rare. There are only around 100 every year. You are much more likely to be struck by lightning than to be attacked by a shark.

DON'T: Shout, splash, or kick legs in the water

Safety at sea

If someone falls overboard into the sea, they should not shout, splash, or kick their legs in the water. Sharks are attracted to noise and movement, and may mistake a splashing person for a school of fish.

Seal or surfer?

Sharks don't seem to like the taste of people. They do not usually eat people they attack.

Perhaps they bite swimmers by mistake—after all, from under the water, a surfer looks a lot like a seal.

Sea drama

Sound travels a long way under water. The noise of people splashing in the sea and the whirr of a rescue helicopter's rotor blades may attract sharks from several miles away.

Sharks in danger

Every year around 100 million sharks are killed. Most of them are killed for their skin, meat, and fins. Some are killed for sport. Others are killed by accident when they swim into fishing nets or shark nets. Some types of sharks take years to have young or may have only one pup a year. If more sharks die than are born each year, they will become extinct.

Made from sharks

Sharks are killed to make creams, medicines, and shark fin soup. Most of these goods can be made using other products.

Death trap

Harmless sharks are sometimes killed in nets put up to protect swimmers from more dangerous sharks.

Shark fin soup is popular in many Asian countries.

Shark liver oil capsules

Skin cream

stick

A shark-tooth necklace is believed to give the wearer strength.

A sporting chance?
Some fast-swimming sharks, such as the mako shark, are the "big game" of the sea.

In the past, many sharks were killed for sport. Nowadays, anglers are encouraged to release them instead.

Studying sharks

Scientists still have many questions about sharks. How long do they live? How fast do they grow? How far do they swim? To help find the answers, scientists clip sonic tags to sharks' fins. The tags give out signals that the scientists can follow. Over the years, scientists have studied thousands of sharks, and are learning more about them. And the more they know, the better chance they have of saving them from extinction.

Spear

Label asking where the shark was caught, its length, and weight

Metal-tipped dart tag

Shark tags

Scientists use long spears to tag sharks in the water. A tag's label asks any angler who catches the shark to send in information about it.

Shark speedometer

Sometimes a tiny propeller is tied to a shark's dorsal fin. The propeller measures how fast the shark moves as it cruises through the sea.

Tagging a shark
Tagging is harmless to
sharks as long as it is done
quickly. In the long run, it
may help protect them
from extinction.

Shark gear

Many divers like to swim with sharks. They have to protect themselves in case they are attacked. Most divers wear special suits made of metal mesh. Some swim inside plastic scooters. To watch or photograph more dangerous sharks, divers stay inside a metal cage. They tie a bag of bait to the bars of the cage—then all they have to do is wait!

Bag of fish for bait

Steel cage

Shark scooter

Motor

Scary but safe

Sharks are attracted by metal, but a steel cage won't break even if it is rammed by a great white shark.

Plastic scooter

This shark scooter is made of strong, clear plastic. The diver can see well and move around freely.

Chain mail hood

Mask

Close-up of a neptunic's steel rings

Underwater armor

In the water divers wear a heavy metal suit called a neptunic. The neptunic is made up of around 400,000 tiny stainless steel rings, which link together to form a fine chain mail. The rings stop a shark's teeth from piercing the skin but won't prevent a nasty bruise.

Scuba gear allows the diver to breathe under water

Chain mail gloves

Wet suit

Flippers

Underwater camera and light

Neptunic diving suit

29

Seeing sharks

You don't have to get wet to see a shark! You can watch one at an aquarium through a wall of glass. Why not sketch, make notes about, or photograph the different types of sharks you see? Of course, an aquarium is too small for large, fast sharks. These fish need a lot of space and are much better off in the open sea.

Making a shark factfile, with notes, photographs, and sketches

An all-around view

Some aquariums have ocean tanks big enough to house whole coral reef. As visitors walk through glass tunnels they enjoy an amazing view of different types of sharks such as smooth hounds, sandtigers, or whitetip reef sharks.

Glossary

...rtilage The rubbery or gristly ...aterial that forms a shark's ...eleton.

...ral reef A long line of coral ...t lies below the water in ...rm, shallow parts of the sea. ...ral is built by tiny animals.

...untershading The name given ...the shading on sharks and ...ny other fish. The darker ...ck and paler belly make them harder to see,

...her ...m above looking down ...o deep, dark water, or from ...ow, looking up toward ...ght sunlight.

...ticles The small, stiff, thorny ...les that make up a shark's ...gh skin.

...inct No longer living ...Earth. An animal ...omes extinct when ...ne of its kind ...live.

...ding frenzy The ...ivity that takes ...ce among feeding

sharks. They become excited, biting at anything.

fish An animal with a backbone that lives in water and breathes through gills. There are around 24,620 known types of fish. Some live in freshwater; some in saltwater. Some, such as the bull shark, can live in both.

gill The part of a fish's body that allows it to breathe under water. Gills take in oxygen from the water. Most fish have gills that are covered with flaps of skin, but sharks just have slits.

luminous Giving out a bright light.

neptunic A diving suit made of thousands of small steel rings. Divers wear a neptunic to protect themselves from sharks.

oxygen A gas that all living things need in order to survive. Oxygen is found in both air and water.

plankton Microscopic plants and animals that live in the sea.

predator A hunter.

prey An animal hunted by another for food.

pup A baby shark.

school a large group of one type of fish.

scuba gear Equipment that includes an air tank and a breathing mask that lets divers breathe under water.

serrated Having a sharp, zigzag edge like a saw or steak knife.

skeleton The frame inside an animal's body that holds it up. Most fish have a bony skeleton, but a shark's skeleton is made of flexible cartilage.

streamlined Having a smooth body shape that moves easily through the water.

Index

Llewellyn, Claire.

The best book of
sharks.

DATE		

DISCARDED BY THE
GLEN COVE PUBLIC LIBRARY